MW01047562

POP CULTURE

STORIES FROM PEPSI-COLA'S FIRST 100 YEARS

BY LEGS McNEIL WITH AN INTRODUCTION BY BRIAN SWETTE

A SPECIAL PREVIEW EDITION FOR THE 1998 CENTENNIAL CELEBRATION AND GLOBAL MEETING

1898

1905

1906

1945

1951

1962

1971

1991

1998

Introduction

Pepsi has sometimes been a mirror to the world, often an amplifier of the times and even a catalyst for change.

When we set out on the centennial book project, we wanted to capture all of that with the same spirit that created one of the world's greatest brands.

So, we came upon the concept of 100 years, 100 stories. After all, everybody loves a good story. In a lot of ways, storytelling is the cornerstone of humanity.

And we've got a great story. In fact, we've got a lot of them.

But we needed a way to weave them together. Along came Legs McNeil. He came back with the idea of tracing Pepsi-Cola's role in the history of pop culture.

I hope you find the first installment as exciting and inspiring as I have.

The full 100 stories will hit the bookstores this summer.

Let's make the next 100 years more exciting than the first.

Credits
Cover: © Alfred Wertheimer, all rights reserved. Elvis and Elvis Presley are Registered Trademarks of Elvis Presley Enterprises, Inc. Cover Art Copyright © PepsiCo, Inc.
Front End; Page 3: © Alfred Wertheimer, All rights reserved. Elvis and Elvis Presley are Registered Trademarks of Elvis Presley Enterprises, Inc.
Page 4: © 1998 Lucasfilms Ltd., All rights reserved.
Page 10: The Pepsi-Cola Collection.
Page 11: Courtesy Archive Photos.
Page 12: The Pepsi-Cola Collection. Card courtesy of Dart Flipcards, Inc.
Page 13: © Ewing Galloway.
Page 14: Top left, right, The Pepsi-Cola Collection. Bottom left, Bob Stoddard Collection.
Page 15: Top left, Jim Downs, for Bob Stoddard Collection. Bottom left, top center, middle center, top right, Bob Stoddard Collection. Bottom center, The Pepsi-Cola Collection. Bottom right, Stewart Sargent, courtesy of Dart Flipcards, Inc.
Page 16-17: Bob Stoddard Collection.
Page 17: Culver Pictures, Inc.
Page 18-19: Bob Stoddard Collection.
Page 20: Jim Bourg, Reuters/Corbis-Bettmann.
Page 20-21: The Pepsi-Cola Collection.
Page 22: Pepsi-Cola Advertising Collection, Archives Center, National Museum of American History, Smithsonian Institution.
Page 23: © 1955 Dennis Stock, Magnum Photos, Inc.
Page 24-25: Courtesy Archive Photos.
Page 26: UPI/Corbis-Bettmann.
Page 27: The Pepsi-Cola Collection.
Page 28: Left, Jim Downs for Bob Stoddard Collection. Right, UPI/Corbis-Bettmann.
Page 29: © Stephen Lynch/IPOL, Inc.
Page 30: Mike Shea, Courtesy of Playboy Enterprises, Inc.
Page 31: © Paul Harris, Outline Press Syndicate.
Page 32-33: The Pepsi-Cola Collection.
Page 33-35: NBC Photo.
Page 36: © Michael Norica, Outline Press.
Page 37: Top, The Pepsi-Cola Collection. Bottom, Henry Ray Abrams, UPI/Corbis-Bettmann.
Page 38-39: Courtesy of National Aeronautics and Space Administration.
Page 40: © Joe Koshollek, the *Milwaukee Journal Sentinel*.
Page 41: © Heather Denman.
Page 42-43: Jim Downs for PepsiCo, Inc.
Page 44: Right, Courtesy of General Colin Powell (Ret.) personal collection.
Page 45: Ray Foli, UPI/Corbis-Bettmann.
Page 46: The Andy Warhol Foundation, Inc./Art Resource, NY.

Written by Legs McNeil
Researched by Don Gilbert and Mary Greening

Designed by Bonnell Design Associates
Design Director: Bill Bonnell
Designer: Peter Roman

Published by Byron Preiss Multimedia Company, Inc.
Project Director: Tim Nolan
Editor: Ruth Ashby
Managing Editor: Michele LaMarca

Photo Editors: Barbara Koppelman and Jim Downs

Special thanks to Howard Zimmerman

Printed in Singapore
ISBN 0-671-01187-1

5¢
Pepsi Cola

the Golden Age of Soda Pop

Cocaine. Opium. Morphine. Alcohol.

Not exactly the ingredients you think of when someone mentions soft drinks. But a hundred years ago, before the 1906 Pure Food and Drug Act was passed, inventors all over America were concocting their own "magic" formulas for soda pop, which, more often than not, contained ingredients that today would be considered highly illegal.

It started innocently enough. When naturally carbonated spring waters were discovered in Saratoga Springs, New York, early American businessmen realized there was money to be made bottling and selling carbonated waters to people who believed in their fantastic curative powers.

By the early 1870s, scientists were able to create artificially carbonated waters in the laboratory, and when an inventor by the name of John Matthews began manufacturing carbonated water machines, soda fountains popped up across America to give the local saloon its first real competition. Overnight, John Matthews had single-handedly invented the soda water drinking industry, and soda pop quickly became an American institution.

Curiously, it was mostly pharmacists who busied themselves making carbonated beverages, and that's where the problems started.

Up through the 1850s, artifically carbonated waters were rather bland, and pharmacists began adding their own roots and herbs, not to make them taste better but presumably to increase their curative powers. Before long, patent medicines and homemade tonics flourished, and over-the-counter preparations containing morphine, codeine, opium, and cocaine were widely available and required no prescription.

Caleb Bradham, a pharmacist in New Bern, North Carolina, was one of these early enthusiastic experimenters. A chatty fellow who was very popular with customers, Caleb Bradham liked to tend the soda fountain in his New Bern drug store and was always busy concocting different tonics to cure his neighbors' "dyspepsia" (indigestion).

One of Caleb's tonics, a mixture of carbonated water, sugar, vanilla, rare oils, and kola nuts, was an instant hit at the soda fountain. Caleb's tonic, called "Brad's Drink" by his customers, proved such a success that Caleb was forced to turn the drugstore over to his assistant so he could work full time on his new soda.

But Caleb Bradham didn't like the label Brad's Drink, even though it was named after him. Taking the "pepsi" out of "dyspepsia," Caleb renamed his drink "Pepsi-Cola" in 1898 and went from selling a few gallons of syrup, which he mixed with carbonated water at his soda fountain, to distributing 7,969 gallons of syrup to fountains throughout the South by 1902. Fueled by the Temperance Movement, which was committed to banning alcohol across the United States, Pepsi-Cola was an immediate success as a refreshing alternative to beer and wine, and by 1909 Caleb found his homemade "tonic" was being manufactured by 250 bottlers in twenty-four states.

Pepsi's initial success was due in large part because of Caleb's insistence that his cola be free of any "special ingredients," found in other sodas of the day.

When President McKinley was assassinated in 1901 and Teddy Roosevelt became the twenty-sixth president, the Gilded Age gave way to the Age of Reform. Partly due to Upton Sinclair's 1906 bestseller *The Jungle,* which exposed the revolting conditions in Chicago's meat-packing houses, and partly due to *Collier's Magazine*'s 1905 series "The Great American Fraud," which exposed the narcotic ingredients in tonics, sodas, and patent medicines, consumers clamored for change on all fronts.

The passage of the Pure Food and Drug Act in 1906 forced many companies to change their product formulas, but not Pepsi. Instead, "Brad's Drink" went on to earn a reputation as the best-tasting cola ever invented, and for the next hundred years continued to live up to the promise of Caleb's 1920 advertising slogan, which told it all: "Drink Pepsi-Cola— It Will Satisfy You!"

Family Business: Caleb Bradham's daughter Mary (left) appeared in one of the earliest Pepsi-Cola advertisements. The fountain at Saratoga Springs in Saratoga, N.Y. (above) is depicted in a mid-nineteenth-century print.

Twelve full Ounces

When the Great Depression almost left Pepsi-Cola bankrupt for the third time, a crazy marketing idea sent sales through the roof!

Loft, Incorporated, the candy company, suffered severe financial repercussions following the stock market crash of 1929. Yet it survived, and thrived, and briefly controlled Pepsi-Cola in the 1930s. During that time, one man and his simple yet brilliant marketing plan turned Pepsi from a liability into an American icon.

Charles G. Guth, who succeeded the late George Loft as the firm's president in 1930, brought with him a reputation as a bold thinker and master salesman. He was also considered by many of his contemporaries to be a tough-minded and unyielding businessman.

Guth found that among the Loft holdings he controlled was a series of candy stores with soda fountains. A dispute with the Coca-Cola Company over bulk prices for syrup led him to make inquiries regarding Pepsi. He learned that he could purchase not only the product but also the Pepsi trademark and assets from out of receivership. After tasting his new acquisition, he insisted Loft chemists improve the formula until he deemed it "about right."

The soft-drink business was highly unstable during those years for any company that didn't have the words "Coca" and "Cola" in its name. Guth soon saw his pet project listing into yet another round of creditors' suits, and realized he had to take some sort of drastic action to keep it from folding.

Prior to 1933, he had concentrated his efforts toward marketing Pepsi through soda fountain sales, almost completely neglecting the handful of bottling operations that worked with Pepsi-Cola. The Mavis Bottling Company in New York's Long Island City bottled Pepsi in the then standard six-ounce container, which retailed for five cents at Loft's candy outlets. Guth decided to make the bottled product more attractive and enticing. In early 1933 he replaced the smaller containers with twelve-ounce, foil-wrapped bottles and made them available to his stores. The "specialty" bottles sold for ten cents, though not in the quantities he had hoped.

Difficult times call for desperate measures. Operating at a loss demanded that costs be offset by an increase in sales. In the midst of a depression such as the country was experiencing, that meant creating a product for retail sale that was as close to irresistible as might be imagined.

The universally accepted price for soft drinks had been five cents for six ounces. Guth already had large quantities of the twelve-ounce bottles—used beer bottles he got at a discount. Why not fill them up and sell them for the same nickel that bought the smaller size?

Sales took off; not with a huge spurt, but with a steady momentum. By June of 1934, the solvency of Pepsi-Cola was assured. Delaware court papers later indicated that "the date of June 30, 1934, is about the date when Pepsi turned the corner. From then on, its success developed in a most gratifying way."

In a time of great hardship, Charles Guth transformed Pepsi from an almost three-times bankrupt loser into a success story by offering the public what they needed the most: value for their money.

A 1938 advertisement (above) promotes a double-sized bottle that provided an attractive alternative to what had previously been primarily a fountain specialty.

More Pepsi Stuff!

Just can't get enough STUFF! More classic Pepsi collectibles.

Amber Bottle
(1905) $1000.
Although Pepsi-Cola began as a fountain drink, Caleb Bradham thought that bottles would eventually be a big part of the soft-drink business. So in 1905, he began offering Pepsi in amber bottles.

Twelve-ounce Cone Top Can
(1949) $150.
Pepsi was still sold in cone top cans in 1949. The shape of the can made it easier to be filled by standard bottling equipment.

Wooden Six-pack Carrier
(1930s) $100.
As refrigerators became more popular in the late 1930s, so did taking home a six-pack of Pepsi-Cola.

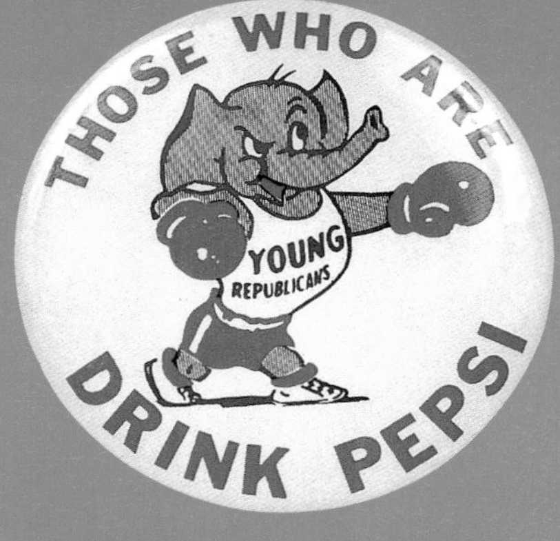

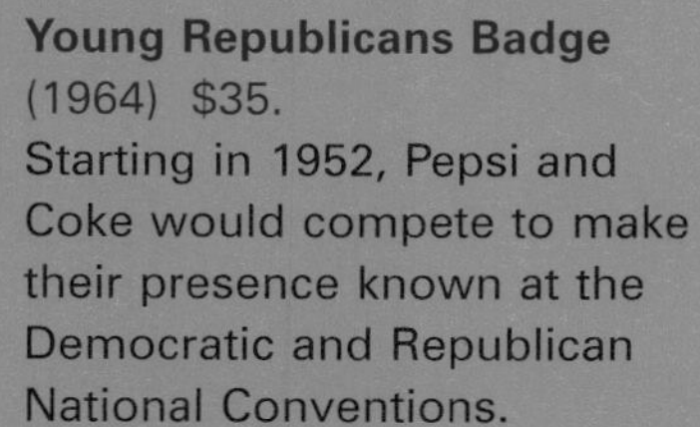

Young Republicans Badge
(1964) $35.
Starting in 1952, Pepsi and Coke would compete to make their presence known at the Democratic and Republican National Conventions.

Musical Lighter
(1951) $100.
Lighting up was accompanied by the Pepsi jingle.

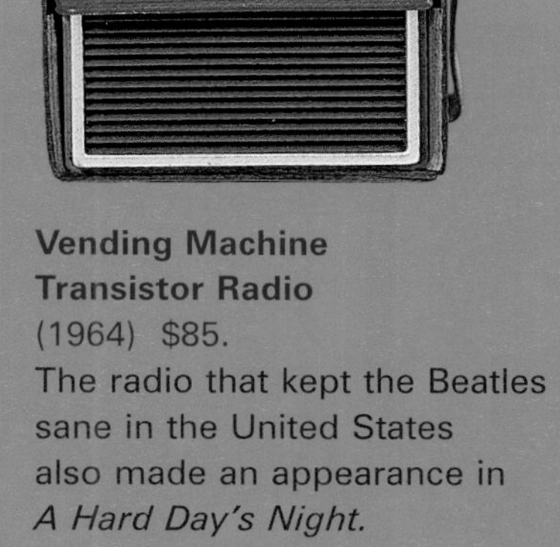

Vending Machine Transistor Radio
(1964) $85.
The radio that kept the Beatles sane in the United States also made an appearance in *A Hard Day's Night.*

Can Transistor Radio
(1970) $10.
Pepsi president Don Kendall used this amusing novelty item to win over Soviet premier Alexei Kosygin.

Syrup Dispenser
(1909) $10,000+.
The 1909 Pepsi-Cola syrup dispenser is the "crown jewel" of Pepsi-Cola collectibles.

Cardboard Sign
(1909) $2,500.
This sign, designed to hang in a soda fountain in 1909, is one of only a few known. It features the "Gibson"-style girl that was popular in advertising at that time.

Buddy L-Comp Wooden Truck
(1943) $700.
Due to war shortages, only the hubcaps could be made of metal.

The Ballad of Pepsi and Pete

I'm Popeye the Sailor Man,
I'm Popeye the Sailor Man,
I'm strong to the finich
'Cause I drinks me . . . Pepsi!
I'm Popeye the Pepsi Man!
(Toot! Toot!)

Can you imagine that everyone's favorite swabby—just after Bluto has locked him in a safe, thrown him off the Golden Gate Bridge, and made off with Olive Oyl—would reach into his shirt and pull out a can of . . . Pepsi in order to make his muscles grow?

If Pepsi-Cola president Walter Mack had had it his way, you might have grown up with your mother saying, "Drink your Pepsi if you want your muscles to grow big and strong like Popeye's," instead of that immortal line from everyone's childhood, "C'mon now and eat your spinach!"

In 1939, Walter Mack tried to buy the rights to the syndicated *Popeye* comic strip so he could pull the old switcheroo and substitute the sailor's super-energizing spinach with Pepsi-Cola.

Gadzooks!

After the rights to *Popeye* were found to be too expensive, Mack got his assistants to scour the countryside for a cartoonist to create the "Pepsi-Cola Cops," whom Mack promptly dubbed Pepsi and Pete. The strip was similar to *Popeye,* in that whenever the pair found themselves in trouble, they overcame the bad guys with energy miraculously supplied by Pepsi-Cola.

Pepsi and Pete ran from 1939 to 1951 and was drawn by the celebrated artist Rube Goldberg, who won millions of fans with his cartoons of elaborate, complex contraptions designed to do simple tasks.

The comic strip featuring the two lovable Pepsi cops grew so popular during the 1940s that actors were hired to dress in Keystone Kop outfits and impersonate Pepsi and Pete at local functions sponsored by Pepsi bottlers.

When Walter Mack was asked, years later, if he regretted not securing the rights to Popeye for his Pepsi comic strip, Mack laughed and said, "No, because Pepsi and Pete did everything we wanted them to do."

Mack might have been content not to have co-opted the spinach-muncher, but you can be sure that generations of kids across America would have preferred their mothers urging them to grow up big and strong by drinking their Pepsi.

Industrious cartoonist Rube Goldberg (right) posed for this 1948 portrait during his tenure as the creator of *Pepsi and Pete*.

Pepsi Pinup: the Petty Girl

Long before Betty Grable, Betty Page, or Farrah Fawcett were best-selling poster girls, the Pepsi pinup had a big following.

It took until the 1990s, but it finally happened. Those forgotten pinup stars of yesteryear are finally being recognized as cultural superheroes and their sultry images as important works of art.

From the turn-of-the-century "Gibson Girl" to Marilyn Monroe to fetish star Betty Page, America has developed a new fascination with the women who sparked our imaginations in poster and magazine art, prompting a re-examination of the pinup as a truly original art form.

In this climate of pinup appreciation, it's important to go back to the beginning, to remember how it all came about; and any history of the modern pinup has to begin with *Esquire* magazine—and the Pepsi-Cola Company.

When *Esquire* began publishing in 1933, it was conceived as a men's fashion magazine that would be distributed mainly to clothing stores throughout the United States, not to newsstands. But that idea quickly went out the window when the first issue, graced with a pinup girl by George Petty, was in such demand that publishers were forced to recall all the magazines from the clothing stores and redistribute them to newsstands in order to keep up with the demand for the "Petty Girl."

As the pinup historian, Mark Gabor, described the phenomenon: "George Petty's famous pinup girl appeared in *Esquire's* first issue — more as a cartoon than a pinup — but the allure of her figure led rather quickly to her development as a singular female type that was destined to become almost as much of a legend as the Gibson Girl had been thirty years earlier."

Just prior to her final appearance in *Esquire,* in December 1941, the Petty Girl briefly went to work for Pepsi. A memo issued by the Pepsi-Cola general sales office on May 17, 1940, announced that "Pepsi-Cola Company has engaged the services of George Petty to paint a series of new illustrations to be used for Pepsi-Cola twenty-four-sheet posters, three-sheet posters, car cards, and other display material. Petty and his work are very well-known throughout the United States, and his daring illustrations appearing in magazines and national advertising have caused widespread comment."

That was an understatement.

Men actually fell in love with Petty's sultry, idealized illustration. One writer tried to describe the effect of her image on himself and a thousand other men: "Every hour she is different. Her demands, her form, the movements of her rippling limbs, the spasmodic play of her wayward moods, give an infinite variety to her spanking beauty. When you tire of her, you tire of life."

As this quote implies, the Petty Girl could be too alluring, and a bit too racy. After one illustration, the campaign was pulled. The Pepsi Petty Girl was gone, but not forgotten. Today she remains among the most sought-after collectors' items among pinup enthusiasts. The car-card, meant to be displayed on trains, streetcars, and buses, shows a "reclining girl with telephone," and features the now famous line,"— but don't forget the Pepsi-Cola."

Time has proven that people haven't forgotten her— or the Pepsi.

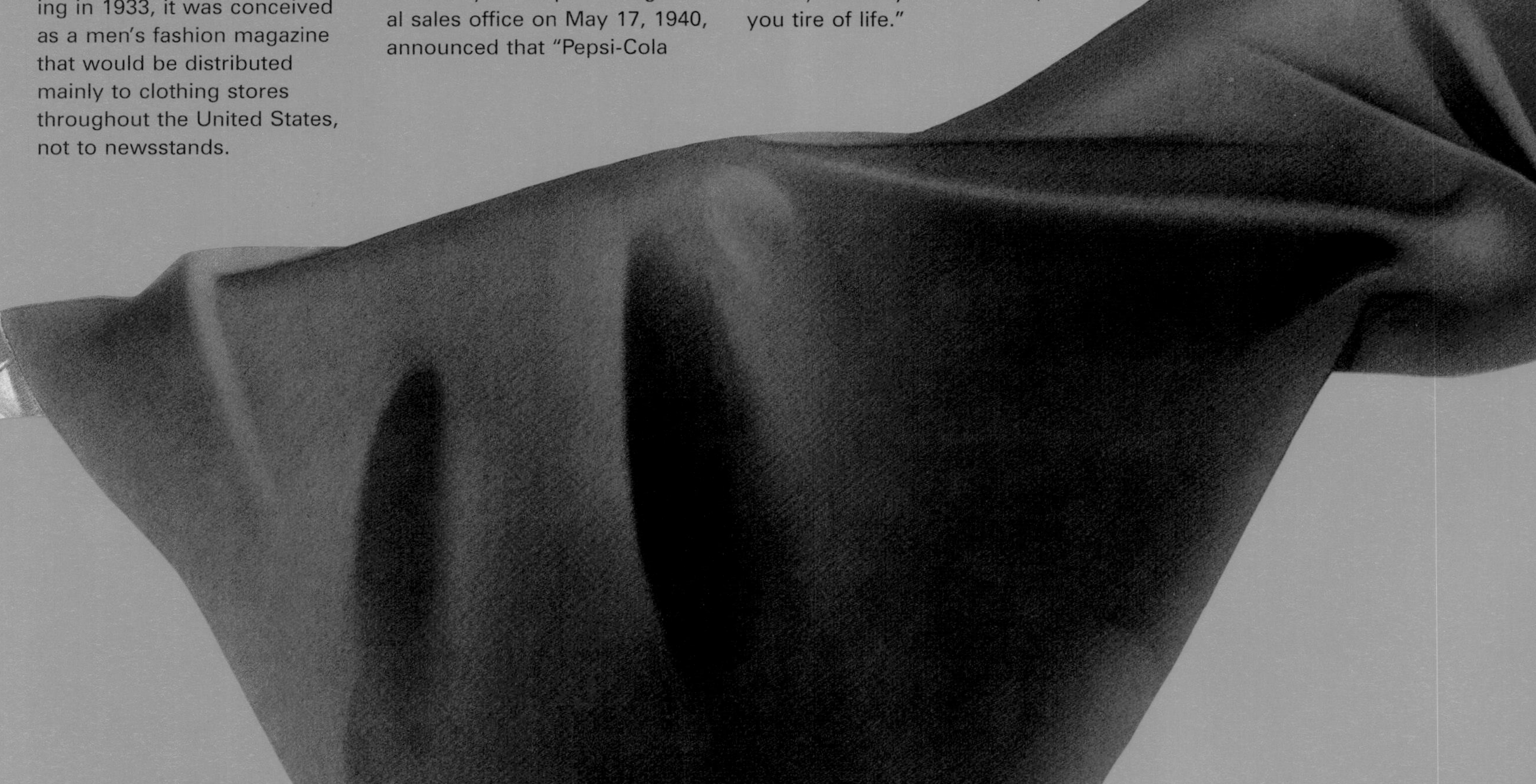

"—but don't forget the
Pepsi-Cola"
A SPARKLING BEVERAGE
Pepsi-Cola
REFRESHING-SATISFYING
12 OUNCES
5¢

Democratic Party Chairman Ron Brown joins President-elect Bill Clinton (above) in Little Rock, Arkansas, following his nomination as secretary of commerce. Brown appeared in a groundbreaking Pepsi ad (right) at age seven.

Shattering the Barriers

Ed Boyd joined the Pepsi-Cola Company in 1946 as one of the first African-American marketing executives in the United States. Among the first young men he hired was Ron Brown, the future secretary of commerce.

In the last year of World War II, the U.S. Army finally became integrated. It was one of the major steps toward civil rights for minorities in America. While it was long overdue, the army's new policy only served to emphasize the deplorable state of race relations on the homefront as troops who had fought side by side, rather than in separate units, returned home to seek jobs or continue their educations.

Just because the U.S. Army had come to its senses didn't mean the civilian world would soon follow suit. But there were some enterprises that welcomed the change, and, in fact, recruited African-Americans for executive positions.

Pepsi-Cola was one of them.

In 1946, Walter Mack hired Ed Boyd to act as the head of the Pepsi Negro Sales Division. Pepsi-Cola, along with Pabst beer and Philip Morris, was among the first companies to employ black sales representatives. Boyd's initial task was to identify promising markets within the black community.

"I couldn't do it by myself," Boyd remembers. "So we developed a team of people that I employed and supervised. Some of them were assigned on a regional basis.

"I was with them on one occasion. We were going from Tuskegee, Alabama, to Montgomery to do a piece of work for one of the bottlers. And we had to go by train.

"You had to eat in the dining car with the curtain drawn. All the black fellows would have to submit themselves to the indiginity of eating behind the curtain. So we would rent a bedroom where the meals were brought to us, so we wouldn't have to eat behind a screen."

Obviously, it was difficult to conduct business under such constraints. But Boyd continued his appeal to the "Negro market" through a series of innovative advertising inserts that featured prominent black Americans, which ran in *Ebony* magazine and select black newspapers throughout the country.

But the problem remained that most large companies wouldn't use African-Americans in their ads for fear of turning off white customers. Ed Boyd finally broke through that barrier when he produced a series of ads for supermarkets to directly support the product on the shelves.

"I wanted something that would portray a natural sort of family gathering and promote Pepsi," Boyd explains. "I knew Ron Brown [later secretary of commerce in the Clinton administration], who was seven years old at the time, and I asked his mother if she would allow him to go to that Pepsi shoot. Ron was always a real precocious little boy.

"We went down to the studio where the ad was photographed. Ron got one dollar. Everyone got one dollar.

"Historically, it was the first piece of advertising actually prepared and designed and conceived as a piece of point-of-sale advertising. It was an immediate success, particularly with the people for whom it was addressed. Nothing like it had been done before."

As *The Wall Street Journal* wrote about the campaign years later, "The campaign was sophisticated, even inspirational. In those days most ads portrayed blacks as caricatures, like Aunt Jemima. Mr. Boyd broke the mold. . . ."

Rebel without a Coke

The James Dean Pepsi commercial.

James Dean cuts up in his first professional acting job in a "Pepsi-Cola Hits the Spot" commercial, 1950.

James Dean represented acting at its most authentic, raw, emotional essence. He will forever be the ultimate alienated youth no one understands. Yet if it weren't for Pepsi-Cola, James Dean might have been just another actor who put on his best performances while waiting tables.

In 1950, when Dean's acting career was going nowhere fast, a friend from UCLA told Dean about a two-minute Pepsi TV commercial he had been hired to act in.

"They need a lot of young people. Why don't you come along?" the friend suggested.

On December 13, 1950, Dean showed up for the Pepsi commercial in L.A.'s Griffith Park, and it turned out to be the big break of his fledgling career. In the commercial, a group of young people are riding the merry-go-round in Griffith Park. Someone pulls bottles of Pepsi from an ice chest and hands them to the teenagers, mostly girls, as they go past the camera on the merry-go-round.

Not exactly Shakespeare in The Park, yet Dean had only been on the set a couple of minutes before the director spotted his good looks and made him the star of the commercial. Dean was cast as the young man handing out the Pepsi to the teenagers.

For another sequence, the director asked if any of the actors could jitterbug. Dean stepped forward, demonstrated his technique, and grabbed that part, too. As the announcer asks, "Say, y'wanna have more fun? Then come on along and let's join the Pepsi crowd!" James Dean, along with the other teens, sings: "Pepsi-Cola hits the spot. / A big, big bottle and it's got, / Bounce, bounce, bounce, / Go get Pepsi for the Pepsi bounce!"

Because Dean could sing and dance, as well as look good on screen, he was the only person on camera during the entire commercial. The pay was twenty-five bucks and a free box lunch. But more important, the commercial was a turning point—it was the pivotal moment James Dean realized he actually could support himself as an actor.

But that wasn't all. Jerry Fairbanks, the producer of the Pepsi commercial, was looking for new faces for a TV movie with a religious theme to be aired on Easter Sunday, called *Hill Number One*. Fairbanks was so impressed with James Dean's good looks and remarkable camera presence that he cast Dean in the part of John the Apostle. The program was shot that February and aired on Easter Sunday, March 25, 1951, on *Father Peyton's TV Theater,* starring Roddy McDowall. Based on his performance in *Hill Number One,* Dean was cast in numerous television shows, usually as the sensitive "religious type." The role that will forever immortalize James Dean, however, was that of the tragically troubled youth in the film classic, *Rebel Without a Cause.*

In a weird coincidence, James Dean returned to the place where it all started for him, Griffith Park, to shoot the famous knife-fight scene in *Rebel.* What is even more strange is that Beverly Long and Nick Adams, two friends of Dean whom he'd first met on the set of the Pepsi commercial, were also cast in supporting roles in *Rebel.*

all shook up

The real story behind Elvis Presley's No. 1 hit.

Elvis Presley was a well-known Pepsi-Cola lover. He drank it everywhere he went; at home in Memphis he had it delivered to Graceland by the case.

Elvis ruled America in 1956. His smash single "Don't Be Cruel" — written for him by composer Otis Blackwell — dominated the pop charts with eleven weeks at No.1 and was clearly the top song of the year.

Blackwell, one of several tunesmiths who supplied the new RCA Victor singing sensation with songs, had sent Elvis a demo of another 1956 composition, "All Shook Up," to be considered for the King's next single.

"All Shook Up" had been inspired by Al Stanton, one of the owners of Shalimar Music, who strolled into Blackwell's workspace one day shaking a cold bottle of Pepsi-Cola.

"Hey Otis," Stanton said with a grin, "why don't you write a song called 'All Shook Up'?" "A couple of days later," Blackwell recalled, "I brought the song in and said 'Look, man, I did something with it!' "

"All Shook Up" was recorded by David Hill for Aladdin Records and by Vicki Young on Capitol, but the song went nowhere. Undaunted, the composer felt the tune would fit his premier client perfectly and provide Presley and Blackwell with yet another shot at the Top of the Pops.

Elvis Presley cut "All Shook Up" at Radio Recorders in Hollywood on January 12, 1957. Issued as both 45-rpm and 78-rpm singles in March 1957, the song entered the charts at No. 25 and within three short weeks shot to No. 1, where it stayed for two full months.

In fact, "All Shook Up" was a hit across the board, topping the rhythm and blues charts for four weeks and reaching No. 3 on the Country chart. It became the first Elvis single to attain No.1 status in England, where it remained at the "Toppermost of the Poppermost" for seven weeks straight.

The song inspired by Pepsi-Cola sold more than 2 million copies and was named Record of the Year for 1957. Its classic status was celebrated by RCA twenty years later when it was included as one of the singles in the boxed sets *15 Golden Records—30 Golden Hits* and *20 Hits in Full Color Sleeves.*

A year later, in September 1958, the newly inducted Elvis was at the Military Ocean Terminal in Brooklyn about to be shipped overseas to Germany. The last song he heard as he boarded the military troop ship was a U.S. Army band saluting him with "All Shook Up."

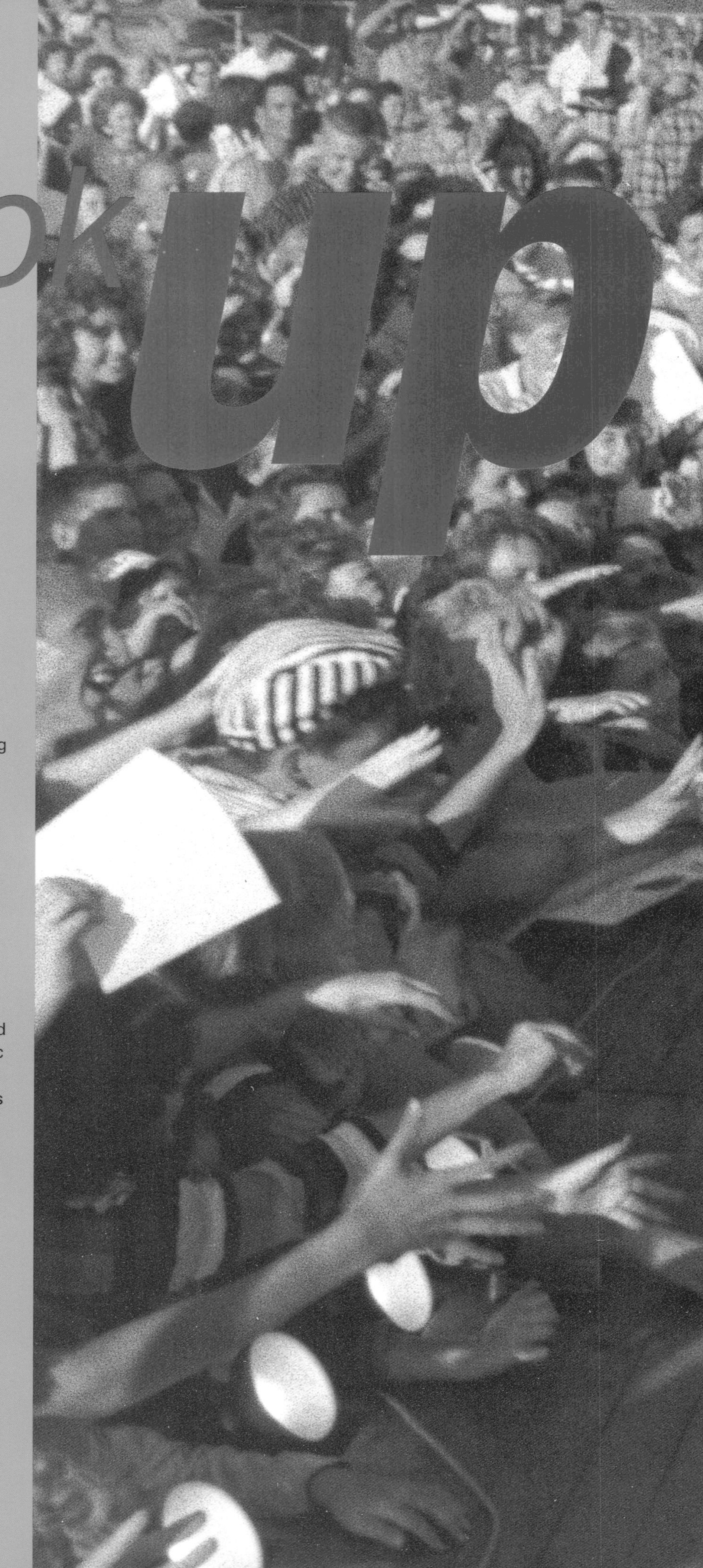

Go, Cat, Go!: Elvis Presley shakes it loose at a county fair in 1956.

Pepsi

Khrushchev gets Sociable!

Truce in the Cold War.

Performing Without a Nyet: International beverage chief Don Kendall pours Pepsi for Soviet Premier Nikita Khrushchev (left) at the American Exposition in Moscow, as Vice President Richard Nixon looks anxiously on, July 24, 1959. The Pepsi proved to be a great hit (above).

It was truly an amazing moment in the history of the tense relationship between the United States and the Soviet Union. During the height of the Cold War, when Russia and America were the bitterest of enemies, someone from the U.S. State Department got the idea to put on a tradeshow, the American International Exposition, in Moscow.

It was the summer of 1959. Both Pepsi and Coke were invited to showcase exhibits, but only Pepsi attended. It was Don Kendall, the head of Pepsi-Cola's international division, who seized the opportunity. He went to Moscow with one objective: to get a bottle of Pepsi into the hands of Nikita Khrushchev. He knew that if he got a photo of the dour, humorless Soviet premier drinking a Pepsi, it would be the publicity coup of the century.

The problem, of course, was how to get the head of the Soviet Union to drink a Pepsi.

The answer came in the form of the vice president of the United States, Richard M. Nixon, who also grasped the publicity value of the Moscow trade show. Nixon was looking to make international headlines of his own, since he planned on running for president the following year against John F. Kennedy, and knew he was going to need all the fanfare he could get in order to compete against Kennedy's charm and good looks.

The night before the opening of the trade show, Kendall met with Nixon and told him of his plan to get a photo of Khrushchev drinking a Pepsi. Nixon assured Kendall that it wouldn't be any problem to bring Khrushchev to the Pepsi booth.

A heated exchange the next day became known the world over as the "kitchen debates," as Nixon and Khrushchev stood in a mock-up of a typical American kitchen, arguing the relative merits of capitalism and communism with this rather ridiculous exchange.

"We're richer than you!" Nixon barked.

"But we are catching up and will surpass you!" Khrushchev countered.

During a break in their arguing for the cameras, Nixon, as promised, took Khrushchev over to the Pepsi booth where Don Kendall had prepared the public relations scheme of a lifetime.

In order to get Khrushchev to try a Pepsi, Kendall had come up with the ingenious idea of presenting the Soviet premier with two bottles of Pepsi: one bottled in the United States and the other one made on site at the Exposition.

The contents of the two bottles were exactly the same, but Kendall asked Khrushchev to sample them both and choose which one he preferred. Under the intense gaze of the international media, Khrushchev guzzled the two drinks and, using the moment for his own propaganda purposes, told the world that the Pepsi made on Soviet soil was the better of the two.

Donald Kendall had gotten his photo. The picture of Nikita Khrushchev, the leader of the Soviet bloc, enjoying a Pepsi, the very symbol of the decadent bourgeoisie, ran all over the world. The caption that was used reflected the Pepsi advertising slogan of the 1950s, "Khrushchev Learns to Be Sociable!"

Meanwhile, back at the trade fair, Khrushchev went on to suck down seven more bottles of Pepsi, heralding a promising future for the soft drink in Russia.

Pepsi Cures the Beatlemania Blues

Victor Bockris, rock 'n' roll biographer, remembers how Pepsi entertained the Beatles during their first American tour:

But You Can't Hear Me: After weeks of being besieged by hysterical, mostly female, fans, the Beatles (above) holler a fond farewell to New York City before skipping back across the Atlantic in 1964.

Do you remember those little transistor radios in the shape of Pepsi vending machines? They were promotional items; I don't know if you could buy them at the store or not, but somehow, Paul McCartney was given one when he arrived in New York City for the Beatles' first American tour, on February 7, 1964.

The Beatles had come to play *The Ed Sullivan Show* in New York, followed by a concert at Carnegie Hall, another one in Washington, D.C., and then two more appearances on *Ed Sullivan* from Miami Beach. They were all looking forward to the tour because it was the first time any of them had been to America. But it was just too crazy!

What was interesting was that they were all naive enough to think they were going to get to see America. No way. They couldn't go anywhere, and when they did, there were always twenty cops around them and hundreds of screaming girls. The fans were just too crazy. John, Paul, George, and Ringo couldn't leave the Plaza Hotel. They couldn't just go out for a walk or go out sightseeing. They were literally prisoners of the mania they had created.

So the Beatles' only link to the outside world, when they weren't posing for pictures or playing music, was this Pepsi transistor radio in the shape of a little vending machine. It really saved them from going bonkers because it was their only form of entertainment, and Paul carried it with him everywhere.

The Beatles would call up the radio stations and ask them to play the Shangri-Las, Ronnie Spector, or a Motown group, and then they'd sit around their room and listen to the songs over that Pepsi radio. Paul even told the newspapers—when some reporter asked what he had done the previous night—Paul said, "Sat in my room and listened to the radio."

And it was very cool looking: a transistor radio shaped like a miniature Pepsi vending machine. It's probably a big collectors' item by now.

BEATLES

What Sort of Man Drinks Pepsi?

(Hugh Hefner, of Course)

Hugh Hefner has been a dedicated Pepsi man for more than half a century. How else do you think he managed to keep up the good life?

"What sort of man drinks Pepsi?" Hugh Hefner asks seriously. "The sort of man who publishes *Playboy* magazine.

"You see, I was raised in Chicago, born in 1926, grew up during the Depression in a middle-class, typical American home with a great deal of repression.

"My mother didn't allow Pepsi or any other colas into the house. So when I started drinking Pepsi, it was probably in reaction to my mother. In fact, my whole life was probably a reaction or overreaction to my Protestant, puritanical, Midwestern upbringing.

"The fifties were the age of conformity," Hefner says. "People wore these tight little gray flannel suits, and they went to their tight little jobs. It was a period of emerging American affluence and the burgeoning of a whole new middle class that hadn't existed before the Second World War. In the fifties, you couldn't talk politically, you certainly couldn't use obscenity in published form, or television or film. And *Playboy* represented a break from all that.

"The magazine started from nothing and was a success from its very first issue, "Hefner remembers proudly. "It was as if it was a moment and an event, waiting to happen.

"After having spent most of the fifties behind the desk creating the fantasy, I really started living out the fantasy. I reinvented myself, probably because I was running as fast as I could to get away from the life I didn't want to live: my parents' life. I just wanted to turn myself and my life into something else.

"That's why I started drinking Pepsi over Coke. Coke represented the establishment and I wanted to be anti-establishment and Pepsi represented something new and different. Pepsi was the underdog, which I liked and related to. Plus, Pepsi had 'twice as much for a nickel, too!'

"Even though *Playboy* precedes the Pepsi Generation by ten years, I think there is a direct parallel between the two because that was the time when the youth market was born.

"The Pepsi Generation started in 1963 and continued through the sixties, which was an incredible time of change. *Playboy* saw enormous growth then. We jumped in circulation from 1 million to 7 million in the sixties. So I'd have to say that the Pepsi Generation really embraced *Playboy.*

"And I, of course, was already drinking Pepsi."

More recently, though, Hefner changed his drink. He's now a Diet Pepsi man, a fact that was noted—somewhat incorrectly—in a popular publication. Hef explains:

"There's a *People* magazine special edition entitled 'The Most Intriguing People of the Century' that came out last year. I'm featured in it. They ran a photo of me from the sixties surrounded by Playboy Bunnies, and the caption reads, 'He didn't do it for sex, he did it because he loved work. He usually fell asleep at his own parties drinking a Diet Pepsi,' which is untrue.

"I never fell asleep at one of my own parties. And I didn't start drinking Diet Pepsi until after my stroke in 1985. Actually, at my parties I was known to enjoy my Pepsi and Jack Daniels."

Bed Partners: Hugh Hefner and his favorite soft drink (left) set up shop in 1955. Above, Hef is surrounded by the fruits of his labor in an undated photo.

Deep in the Heart of Texas

Launching the great Pepsi counterattack, or the Pepsi Challenge, Part One.

It was the showdown of the century: two of the oldest and most bitter rivals in the world, standing belly to belly, cold sweat pouring down their necks, each one foaming at the mouth, battling it out for the title of the best cola ever. It was another round in the marketing heavyweight championship of the world.

The Pepsi Challenge originated in 1972, as an in-store promotion in which consumers were asked to try each of two unidentified soft drinks and to choose the one they found tastier. The compiled data produced a compelling victory for Pepsi, but only as long as the competing colas remained unnamed. The Pepsi brain trust believed this was potentially explosive information, and after they considered all aspects of the situation, they decided they had only one course of action: total, all-out comparative war.

The Atlanta-based Coca-Cola Company had a stranglehold on many markets below the Mason-Dixon line, and no locality was supposed to be more indifferent toward Pepsi than the great state of Texas. In the Dallas-Fort Worth area, Pepsi sales lagged almost three-to-one behind Coke. Pepsi-Cola saw the public relations value of flinging down their gauntlet deep in the heart of enemy territory and, in 1975, deployed a guerrilla ad production team to record and process the results of the newly christened Pepsi Challenge.

"Pepsi-Cola!" the good old boy yipped in the first Pepsi Challenge commercial. "I'll be darned. Well, I've got to go. Millie's waiting for me."

As labels marked "Q" and "M" were peeled off the bottles to reveal which was Coke and which was Pepsi, Coke issued statements maintaining that they had conducted research proving that Pepsi had rigged the tests by labeling its product with the letter "M," which people found to be more psychologically comforting than the oddly formed "Q."

Coke's unusual claim spurred the Pepsi advertising agency, BBDO, to switch the taste test letters to "L" and "S." Coke countered with a spoof advertisement, ridiculing the Challenge concept, by asking "consumers" to explain why they preferred the letter "L" to "S."

Unfortunately for Coke, their counteroffensive proved ineffectual. What's more, as the Pepsi Challenge kept on coming, the taste test revealed an unexpected side effect: not only, as the tag line stated, did "more people prefer the taste of Pepsi to Coke" but also many older, stalwart Coke consumers, well outside the demographic range of the Pepsi Generation that Pepsi had targeted with their life-style campaigns, had given the challenger their thumbs up.

"Grandma picked Pepsi!" a little girl shouted as the brands were revealed in another commercial. "I can't believe it," said Grandma. "I've drank Coke all my life."

Amazingly, Pepsi even began to achieve substantial sales gains in Texas. When John Sculley became president of Pepsi in 1977, he implemented a master plan to expand the Pepsi Challenge to a national scale. Local Pepsi bottlers across the country would set up Challenge booths in public venues and film the taste tests. Eventually nearly 300 communities from New York to Hawaii had their own "personalized" Pepsi Challenge commercials, featuring recognizable friends and neighbors.

Publicly, Coke adopted the tactic of belittling Pepsi by name, a first for the company that up until that point dared not speak its competitor's name. Privately, they conducted clandestine taste tests, which led to one indisputable conclusion: to many people, Pepsi really did taste better.

The Pepsi Challenge had Coke on the ropes. For the first time in its history, Coke was running scared. So scared that deep in the secret labs of Coca-Cola, teams of professional cola "doctors" began to revamp Coke's original formula to make it taste more like Pepsi.

The Pepsi Challenge campaign (above and right) proved that consumers preferred the taste of Pepsi to Coke in blind taste tests conducted in staunch Coke strongholds.

Coca-Cola
PEPSI

"no Coke; Pepsi!"

The John Belushi Pepsi story.

Believe it or not, one of the world's favorite TV comedy sketches was inspired by the "cola wars" trademark infringement battle. In the late seventies, Coca-Cola stepped up its efforts to keep "Coke" from becoming a generic term by releasing its Trade Research Department on an unsuspecting world. A team of about twenty-five investigators ordered "Coke" and "Coca-Cola" in restaurants and diners across America, took samples of what they were served, and then sent the evidence to their corporate headquarters in Atlanta for chemical analysis.

God help the poor counterman who served any other cola when the investigators made their order. Busted by the Coca-Cola Cops!

Just at the time Coke was bringing case after case of alleged trademark infringement to court, involving restaurants that had served another cola when asked for "a Coke," a new team of comedians were shaking up late-night television and making comedic history with their over-the-edge humor on *Saturday Night Live.*

One of the main writers of *SNL* was Don Novello, who was also regularly featured on the show as Father Guido Sarducci, a gossip columnist from Vatican City. John Belushi, a main star of *Saturday Night Live,* had returned to the show after filming his first movie, *Animal House,* which was destined to make him a bona fide movie star. Belushi was hanging around the NBC studios with Novello and happened to tell the writer about his father's old restaurant and how all the waiters had to make sure to tell the customers they only had Pepsi when someone asked for a Coke, lest the Coca-Cola Cops bust the place.

Novello thought it was a great idea for a sketch and, the next thing you know, he had developed a long skit about a small Greek restaurant called the Olympia, with a limited menu and no substitutions.

None.

Bob Woodward, in his best-selling biography of John Belushi, described what happened next:

"On January 28, 1978, the show opened on a short-order diner with a few swivel stools and fewer customers. John, the management, is in a white shirt, sleeves rolled up, a thin black tie. He has the absent gaze of the assembly-line worker until Jane Curtin orders a tuna salad sandwich.

"'Nope,' he snaps, order book poised. 'No tuna. Cheezbugga? . . . Cheezbugga? Comma, comma, comma . . . we ain't got all day. Cheezbugga? Comma, comma. Whadda ya gonna have?'

"Curtin makes a few attempts. No luck. A Coke?

"'No Coke," John says. 'Pepsi.' "

Within days, across America, the catchword of the moment became Belushi's rallying cry, "No Coke; Pepsi!" And it looked like, for the time being, Pepsi had won this round of the cola wars.

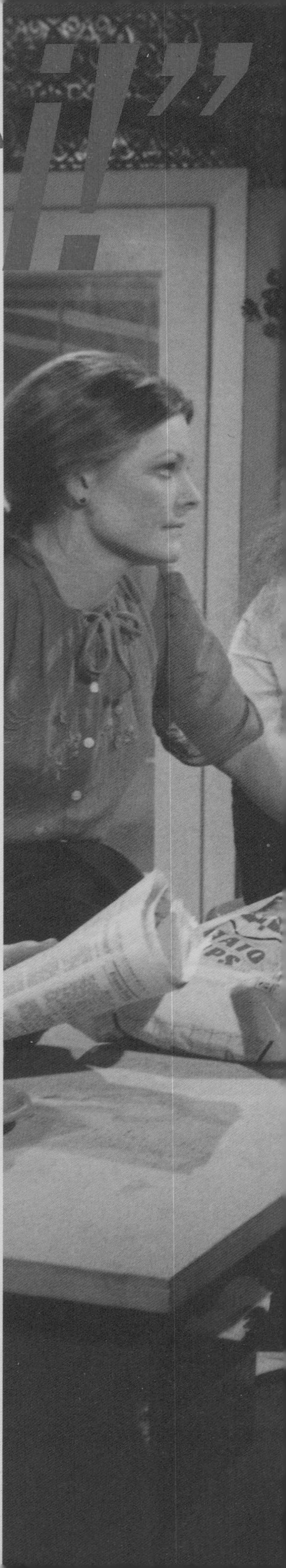

Short Order: Jane Curtin, Gilda Radner, John Belushi, Bill Murray, and Dan Aykroyd deal with the limitations of the Olympia's lunch counter.

Back in the mid-1980s, we signed what became a highly publicized contract with pop singer Michael Jackson. It was before the major controversies about Michael, but even then it was a pretty controversial deal.

He was not your everyday corporate-sponsored celebrity. He looked unusual, to put it mildly, wearing a kind of studded military uniform with one white glove. His nose and complexion seemed odd, suggesting plastic surgery. He spoke a little like Jackie Kennedy.

But it wasn't his appearance that caused the controversy. It was the size of his contract. We paid him a breathtaking $5 million to appear in a couple of commercials and to sponsor his upcoming Victory Tour. This was ten times more than anybody had been paid before for this kind of thing and probably ten times more than anybody has been paid since.

Foolish? Lots of people thought so. Driving to work one day, I heard Don Imus call me the "dumbest man on earth."

But we still had confidence in the deal. To those of us familiar with the economics of big brand advertising, it was a bargain. You see, each year we spend hundreds of millions to buy television time, for one purpose: to make Pepsi the most exciting, contemporary, youthful product in the world. And that's no small trick when your product is one hundred years old.

Michael had suddenly become the most famous entertainer in the world. His 1982 record album, *Thriller,* was the best-selling album, ever. We figured that if Michael could make our commercials 10 or 20 percent more exciting, more anticipated, more talked about, we would double the value of our media money, at a minimum. Plus we could promote our products around the tour and barter all of those hard-to-get concert tickets. We saw a more than $20 million value in Michael and the tour—if we did it right.

The secret, of course, was to create great commercials. Our goal was to produce the most highly publicized, powerful advertising in the history of soft drinks. We intended to make them so good that consumers would tune into a TV show just to see the Pepsi/ Jackson commercials.

It started out great. Michael volunteered his very popular song, "Billy Jean," as our theme music. We hired the best director and best choreographer, wrote great Pepsi lyrics, had wonderful story boards. We built the perfect set.

Even a near disaster added to the interest and excitement. On the last day of shooting, a spark from a fireworks display alighted on Michael's gelled hair and huge flames shot up. He was rushed to the hospital, pursued by dozens of news cameras. We were lucky: although painful, the burn was superficial. There was no permanent damage, but the new publicity created even more anticipation.

We decided to premiere the spots at a black tie extravaganza at Lincoln Center. Hundreds of TV stations planned to run brief clips of the commercial during the day. MTV agreed to telecast a special preview.

A week before the first showing, consumer awareness had climbed so high that we had become the best-known commercials in the world and we hadn't spent a dime of media money. What do you mean, a $20 million value? We began thinking $50 million!

A week before the big event, our advertising agency carefully edited the footage into what we all considered two wonderful commercials. They confidently showed them to Michael for approval. Michael said no.

No?

Yes, he said no. All of a sudden we had a very big problem, and my learning experience began.

Nobody had been paying much attention, but since the start of the relationship Michael had insisted that very little of his very well-known face appear in the commercials. His contract called for a total of only two-and-a-half seconds on camera. How he picked two-and-a-half seconds nobody knew, but that's what he wanted, and he had final approval of what went on the air.

Our team never took that demand seriously, figuring that once Michael saw the high quality of the commercials, plus how great he looked, he would change his mind.

He didn't. Then for four days the agency and Michael battled, and I agreed with the agency. We would have to be pretty stupid to pay $5 million for two-and-a-half seconds. Michael argued that the less he appeared, the more interesting and exciting the commercials. Oh, yeah!

To make a long, painful story short, Michael won. We caved in. And guess what? The commercials turned out to be fabulous, the most successful advertising we had ever produced. For six months, they were the most popular on TV. At one point, we actually had to run ads telling consumers when a commercial would appear.

And most importantly, Pepsi sales soared.

So what did I learn? You don't need to be heavy-handed to do a great commercial. Subtlety can be a good thing. Don't beat an audience to death. A flash of sequined glove can be more effective than twenty seconds of talking heads. And if a great performer at the top of his game tells you how to film something, pay attention.

Funny thing. A few years ago, I told this story to PepsiCo's founder, Don Kendall. He smiled in agreement and said he learned the exact same thing from the great Walt Disney. It was back in the fifties, and Disney's new theme park was about to open in Anaheim. Don agreed to sponsor one of the first shows, but he wanted to put a Pepsi logo on the front curtain. He's not the kind of guy to hide his light under a bushel. Walt talked him out of it, saying, "Don, a little subtlety goes a long way."

Walt was right. It really does.

The inimitable Michael Jackson performs (top right) and announces the extension of his personal services contract with Pepsi in 1992 (right).

What Michael Jackson Taught Me about Advertising:

PepsiCo CEO Roger Enrico reveals what he learned about advertising from Michael Jackson.

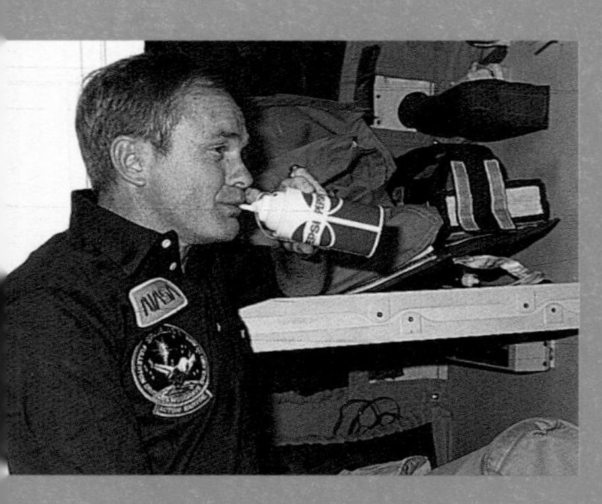

Globule Warming: Major General Roy D. Bridges, ret., (above) piloted the first cans of Pepsi into space aboard the shuttle *Challenger*. Mission specialist Dr. Henize demonstrates how to operate the space can and enjoy Pepsi in the absence of gravity (bottom right).

In 1985, during the training for our mission on the space shuttle *Challenger,* we were introduced to a so-called high-tech carbonated beverage can that Coca-Cola had created in their laboratories.

The experiment was to see if they could create a carbonated taste without a froth, and afterwards there was going to be some evaluation of how well it worked.

Not to be outdone, Pepsi-Cola proposed that they fly their own can on board, and it was accepted. It looked kind of like a whipped cream spray can; of course, it had the Pepsi logo on the side of the can. And when you pushed the nozzle the soda just squirted out. But the fluid was fairly frothy.

Once we took off and got into space, we actually had a lot of fun with the Pepsi because what happens to soda pop in zero gravity is that you'll get a blob of fluid that is held in a spherical shape by the surface tension, and it floats around the cabin.

And within that bubble, that big ball, will be lots of little bubbles. And if you let these balls go, they will start floating around the cabin, too. And if you blow on them, you know, to keep them from hitting the walls or something, they will start rotating, like a little globe, and as they rotate, the fluid will separate out at the middle in an equatorial bulge.

If you think of how the earth was formed, the Pepsi balls do the same thing; the bubbles will go to the north and south poles. And it actually looks like a little world with little north and south polar caps.

Since the bubbles are white, they look like little polar ice caps. So we made a little galaxy of these things, marshaled them around the cockpit for a while and then, of course, we gobbled them down.

But you have to remember that we didn't have refrigeration in space, and you know, for Americans not used to a room temperature beverage, hot pop just isn't the best way to drink it. Other than that, Pepsi in space tastes just like Pepsi. It was just like good old Pepsi.

"Houston, we've got

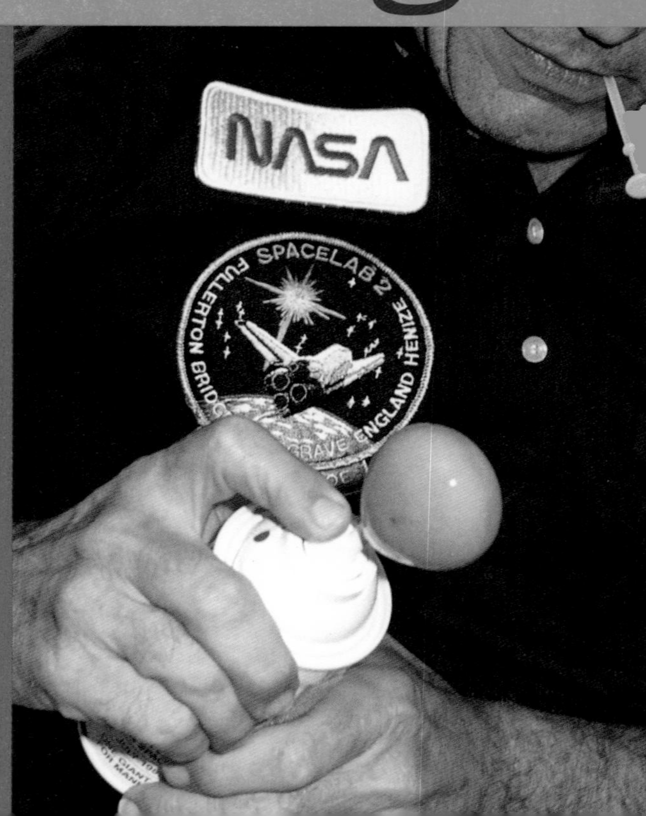

Retired former astronaut and space shuttle pilot Major General Roy D. Bridges remembers how it felt being the first man to drink Pepsi in space.

a problem: "we Need more Pepsi up here in Space!"

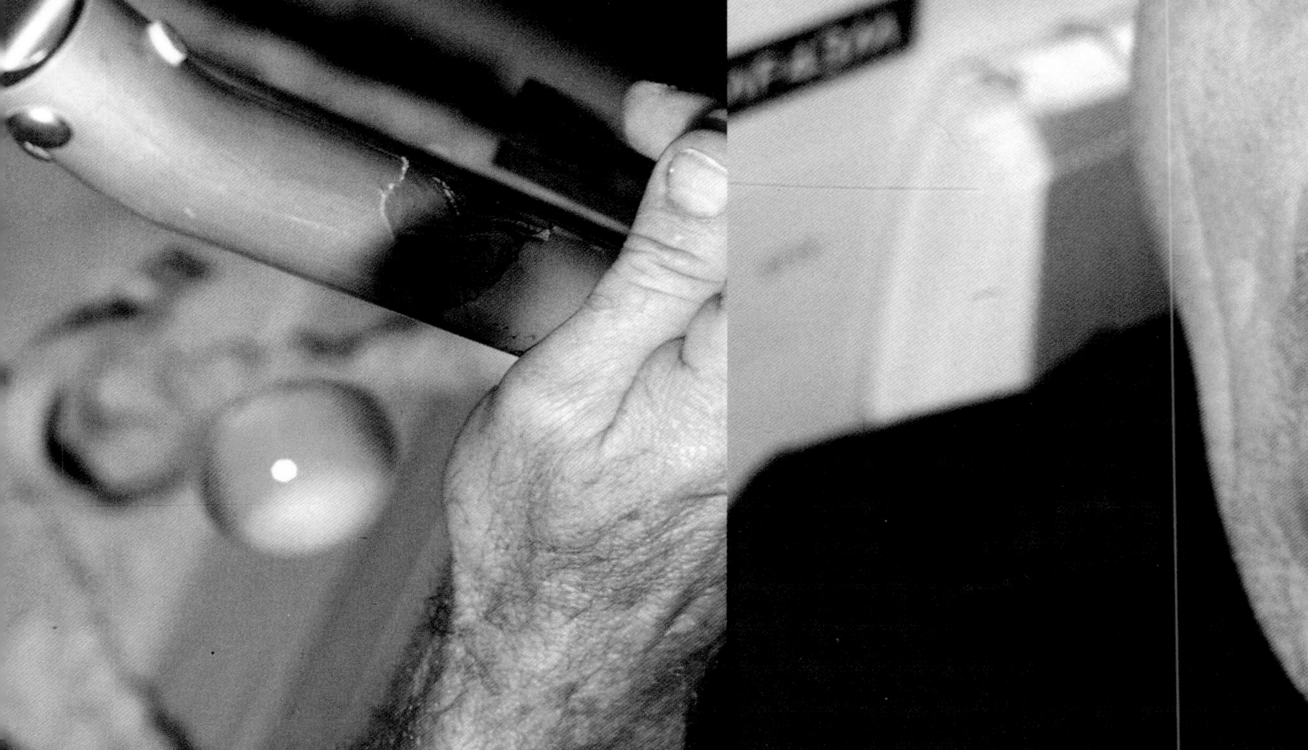

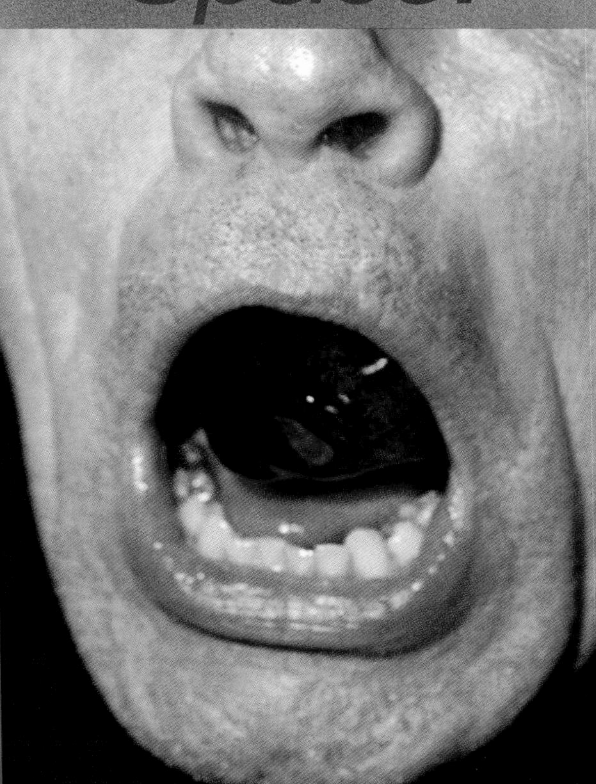

the coolest room in the World!

Milwaukee teen Heather Denman didn't know that when she began redecorating her bedroom with empty Pepsi cans it would lead to a brand-new embassy position: ambassador to GeneratioNext.

"I started collecting Pepsi cans, I guess, because it reminds me of the good times I've had with my friends and my family," Heather remembers. "You know, when I was really young I'd stay up late at night with my dad and watch talk shows like *David Letterman* and stuff, and I would drink Pepsi. So when I started collecting the empty Pepsi cans, I just thought it was a really cool thing.

"The problem was that I used to just stack the empty cans in my room but like when a truck drove by and shook the house, they'd all fall down. So then I started duct taping them to the wall to keep them up there, and before I knew it, I was going all the way around the room.

"I didn't drink them all myself. My friends helped me a lot. And in the end, I had 7,000 Pepsi cans decorating my bedroom. Well, Pepsi found out about me because *Seventeen* magazine had a coolest rooms contest and I typed up an essay about my room and sent in some photos and I won. I was a runner-up. I think I got beat by some girl from Ontario, who had waves painted on her bedroom walls.

"How lame is that?

"Anyway, so there was a picture of my room in *Seventeen* magazine, in the April 1996 issue. When the magazine came out, you know, it got around school and everything, and I really thought I was pretty cool.

But then this producer, Borka Kalahn, from a local talk show out of Madison called *Talk Box,* saw the picture of my room in *Seventeen,* and she called me up and said they were doing a show on cool rooms and asked me to be on it.

"So they came to my house and filmed me in my bedroom and then I went to their studio and answered questions from a live audience.

"It was pretty fun.

"After *Talk Box* aired, my guidance counselor at high school sent Jon Harris, the PR guy from Pepsi, a copy of my appearance on the *Talk Box* show, and he watched that and they thought, 'Wow! She could just be the ambassador of GeneratioNext.'

"So he decided to invite me to come out to a commercial shoot in L.A.

"But I didn't know about it. I came home from work during my lunch break from Berstead's Pick and Save, a grocery store where I work as a checker, and there was a message on the answering machine from Jon Harris, and he just said he wanted to get in contact with me.

"So I called him right away, and he said, 'We watched your video and we think it's really great and how would you like to come to L.A.?'

"I was like, 'Oh my God!'

"We had, like, two days' notice. So I took my mom along with me. It was a nice Mother's Day gift. We took off on Monday morning and Pepsi had a limo waiting for us. And a limo driver named Craig. Then they put us up at the Regent Beverly Wilshire Hotel, and it was really awesome. And it was just, you know, the best hotel room I've ever been in.

"They had, like, you know, limos and Lincoln Town Cars driving us around L.A. for a couple days. And then we hung out at Universal Studios and watched Deion Sanders, Shaquille O'Neal, Picabo Street, Mia Hamm, Holly McPeak, and Jeff Gordon film this Pepsi commercial.

"Yeah, so I talked to everybody.

"Since then I've been photographed by the *National Enquirer* and *Dateline* sent a cameraperson here and so I'm gonna be their picture of the week.

"I just graduated from high school, but I'm planning on going to the local campus here—UWC Richland—so I'll probably live at home for a while. So my room is safe for at least a couple more years.

"After that, I think my mom will probably let me keep the cans up there as long as I want to.

"Maybe that will, like, make me want to come home more."

Bubbling Enthusiasm: Milwaukee's Heather Denman has a soft spot for Pepsi.

PEPSI

"Hey Dude, you said there would be Pepsi in the dressing room?"

Professional rock 'n' roll roadie Timmy Chunks won't go on tour with bands unless they provide him with Pepsi in the dressing room. When one band reneged on its promise, Timmy took matters into his own hands.

Pepsi-Cola Ink: Timmy Chunks took on some legwork (above) and got Pepsi Man tattooed on his arm (right), as a means of displaying his fierce loyalty to the brand.

Blown fuses, broken strings, bulky speaker cabinets, and bogus bass sound are just a few of the hassles touring technicians face each night. But for Timmy Chunks, one of L.A.'s most sought-after road dogs, these are minor inconveniences compared with a dearth of proper refreshments.

So Timmy took matters into his own hands and provided his employers with a potent reminder of his fierce loyalty to Pepsi. As Chunks tells the story:

"I was on tour with Pennywise, a punk-rock band from California. And whenever I go on tour with anybody, my verbal contract is that I have to have Pepsi in the dressing room.

"And they didn't seem to think that it was that necessary. So it became a big joke; they were like, 'Oh, come on, just drink Coke. It's the same thing.'

"And I would say, 'No, it's not the same thing. You're obviously not serious about your soft drinks if you don't care which one you drink.'

"So it would go on and on, back and forth, and then finally, just to prove how serious I was, I got the Pepsi logo—the red and blue circle—tattooed on my leg. And normally where it would say 'Pepsi' it says 'Chunks.'

"We were in Mesa, Arizona. And the guy who was the owner of the club they played in owned the tattoo parlor and a skateboard shop. One of the guys invited the band down to get tattooed or to go to the skate shop and get whatever they needed. Happens a lot when you're with bands.

"So they offered some free tattoos and I went down and I said, 'All right, this is what I need.'

"He was like, 'Really? Is that what you want? Really?'

"And I said, 'Yeah.'

"It was a young kid who did the tattoo and he was just, like, 'OK, whatever you want.'

"It took him about an hour and a half, maybe two hours, tops. The band came in before it was finished and they were just kind of like, 'You're crazy.'

"From then on they provided me with Pepsi. I mean, people don't believe me when I tell them that it's all I drink. I've drunk Pepsi my whole life, and then as the years went on, I became more serious about it. I'm drinking some Pepsi right now.

"Do you know Pepsi Man? He's Pepsi's marketing device in Japan. I wanna get a big Pepsi Man on my arm, like eight inches long or something. Yeah, I wanna get Pepsi Man tattooed on me."

A few weeks later, in New York City, Timmy Chunks got his new Pepsi Man tattoo. Now, let's see anyone try to serve him a cola other than Pepsi!

PEPSI

All Work is Honorable:

General Colin Powell

Fresh from a ticker-tape parade down Broadway for Gulf War heroes, General Colin Powell was invited to throw out the first ball at Yankee Stadium. While driving back into the city, General Powell experienced a private Pepsi moment:

"I rode down the East River Drive and gazed at a huge Pepsi-Cola sign across the river. Suddenly, I was a kid again, swinging a mop across the floors of the Pepsi bottling plant. "

"When I reported to work the first day, I was handed a mop, an experience that black workers have had for generations. I noticed that all the other porters were black and all the workers on the bottling machines were white.

"I took the mop. If that's what I had to do to earn sixty-five dollars a week, I'd do it. I'd mop the place until it glowed in the dark. Whatever skill the job required, I soon mastered. You mop from side to side, not back and forth, unless you want to break your back. It could be godawful work, as it was the day fifty cases of Pepsi-Cola bottles came crashing down from a forklift and flooded the floor with sticky soda pop.

"At the end of the summer, the foreman said, 'Kid, you mop pretty good.'

"'You gave me plenty of opportunity to learn,' I told him.

"'Come back next summer,' he said. 'I'll have a job for you.' Not behind a mop, I said. I wanted to work on the bottling machine. And the next year, that is where he put me. By the end of the summer, I was deputy shift leader and had learned a valuable lesson. All work is honorable. Always do your best because someone is watching."

Parade Dress: General Colin Powell (right) and returning troops were welcomed home following the Persian Gulf conflict with a series of parades in major cities throughout the country. In 1953, one year before he entered college, Colin Powell was photographed near Hunts Point in the Bronx (above).

POWELL
6 MARIST H

Pepsi-Cola
say "Pepsi please"
CLOSE COVER BEFORE STRIKING
AMERICAN MATCH CO., ZANSVILLE, OHIO